LIVING
from the
UNSEEN

reflections from a transformed life

Wendy Backlund

www.ignitinghope.com

Acknowledgements

Cover & Interior Design: Lorraine Box (PropheticArt@sbcglobal.net)
Editing: Steve Backlund, Kim McGan, Julie Mustard
Special Assistance: Maureen Puddle

ISBN: 978-0-9854773-6-3

DEDICATED TO

My husband, Steve

For his encouragement and belief in me

My friends

Cyndi Barber, Berta Johnson, Maryann Perdue and Sue Scott

Thank you for going on the journey with me

"The Interns"

Melissa Basch, Holly Hayes and Kim McGan

*Thank you, for laboring with me and making
my dream come true!*

FOREWORD

There is nobody I respect more than my wife, Wendy. She is an incredible woman who has had a radical transformation in her life that is revealed in *Living From The Unseen*. I have seen first hand the effect of the encounters and revelations upon her that she shares about in this book. Her supernatural experiences with God's love, God's Word, and with the Holy Spirit have changed her before my very eyes. It is truly astounding what has happened to her.

Living From The Unseen is not just a good read, but it will create an open heaven for the reader to see into and receive from the Spirit realm as never before. You will not just have your mind renewed, but your spirit will also receive directly from God. This is a book to be experienced, not just studied.

Get ready for increased hope and practical keys for personal victory. These spiritual gold nuggets will cause an increased understanding of the power of the gospel and bring massive hope for change. Prepare yourself for a gift of faith that will release the supernatural in you and through you like never before. I declare that you will never be the same again!

Steve Backlund

TABLE OF CONTENTS

INTRODUCTION

I n this book I have compiled a collection of revelations that have dramatically changed my life and perspective. These revelations have not changed my theology as much as they have given life and manifestation to the beliefs I already embraced.

For many years, my life did not measure up with my theology, and I thought there was something uniquely wrong with me or that I was the exception to the promises and statements of what a believer looked like. I did not always fit into the usual church ministries and often felt guilty for not enjoying prayer meetings or passing out tracts. I found it difficult to enjoy the limited options of how to pray, serve and conform. My perception of what a good Christian looked like seemed heavy, hard, and impossible! I had a powerful encounter with Christ in the 1970's, but by the late eighties, I was simply going through the motions and trying to please God by works and tears. By the time renewal hit in the nineties, I was ready for change! For many, the renewal was a time of fresh encounters and supernatural signs and wonders. For me, it was a time of life-altering revelations. I never realized how much of the Word was just a mental assent of truth or just watered down to fit into my life experience. I was definitely not experiencing an abundant life – or an overcoming one either! My idea of success was coping with life with a good attitude and not forsaking the faith.

This book represents my journey of searching for the abundant life Jesus preached about. For too long, I tried to transform my life through dying to myself and performing. I was embracing grace and power as a theology, but was clueless as to how to make it work for me. My heart aches with empathy for unmotivated Christians who, at one time, were willing to die for Christ, but are now numb, going through the motions of Christianity, or are simply burned out. Often times, they have been taught to sacrifice all they have and die to themselves; however, since this is only half of the message of Christianity, they feel as if something is missing or something is wrong with them. Jesus did not die on the cross so we might die, but so that we might live (John 10:10)! We must discover what a resurrected lifestyle looks like, and then passionately pursue that supernatural way of life. Believing that these things are available and determining to find the keys for releasing them are both vital for anyone who wants to experience everything Jesus gave us through His death and resurrection. We must recognize what God has put in us before we will be able to utilize and release it.

We are first and foremost a spirit living in a natural body – learning to see, hear, and access the spirit realm and its principles. In my experience, learning to live life through the eyes of the spirit has been transforming and freeing. You might want to adjust to the fact that this book is not written to your mind but to your spirit. If we are to worship Him Spirit to spirit, then perhaps we need to **move from a *theology* of our spirit nature to a clear awareness of our spirit and its potential.**

I passionately desire to see and make others aware of the spiritual realities and principles that are affecting our everyday lives. Many of us are aware of the dark forces and evil powers that can influence lives; however, my goal is to make us aware of an even more powerful influence residing within us – which is affecting the atmospheres and lives of everyone around us. This influence increases as we become aware of what we carry and attach more faith to our ability to impact the world. Perhaps, when Christians move beyond just trying to die to themselves and begin to learn how to live as partakers of the divine nature, we will see the true revealing of the children of God. *"For the earnest expectation of the creation eagerly waits for the revealing of the sons of God"* (Romans 8:19).

PRELUDE

ecause these revelations naturally fell into four different categories, I grouped them into four sections for ease of reading. All of these revelations have allowed me to see the supernatural as attainable and inherent in the normal Christian life. Instead of trying to capture the unseen realm, these truths have helped me to live from the unseen. Although I am not yet walking in all the fullness of these revelations, I am content with the process and rejoice in knowing what I am becoming. My prayer is that all who touch this book or read it will be radically transformed by the revelation of our good and empowering God who is calling all His children into an abundant and fruitful life.

Romans 12:2 says the way to transformation is through renewing the mind and when the Gospels use the word "repent," it's derived from the Greek word *metanoeo*, which basically means to *change the way you think*. Since I have started the journey of changing the way I think and see, my life has dramatically changed and prospered. My prayer is that this book will encourage you on your journey and bring an awareness that the Kingdom is within reach.

To get the most out of this book, I recommend that the reader has a notebook on hand to either journal or apply the applications at the end of each teaching. I have set this book up to also be easily adapted for a Bible study group with applications for each truth.

LIVING FROM
THE SPIRIT

This section is based on the revelation of our identity as new creatures, a new race of beings, born of the Spirit. Once we are born again, we are just as radically altered as the human race was when Adam sinned (Romans 5).

John 3:6 says, "*That which is born of the flesh is flesh, and that which is born of the Spirit is spirit.*" Although many can quote this verse, few can really see themselves as more spirit than flesh.

Many believers are not aware that they are new *creatures born of the Spirit,* which means they have become more spirit than flesh. The part of us that will exist for all eternity is spirit. If we can become more aware of that part of ourselves and allow it to have a voice, then perhaps we could actually see what walking in the spirit could look like. Once, while praying for something supernatural to happen to me or through me, I felt God say, "Wendy, the supernatural is not something that happens to you, but it is something you are." 2 Peter 1:4 says, "*By which have been given to us exceedingly great and precious promises, that through these you may be partakers of the divine nature, having escaped the corruption that is in the world through lust.*" According to the Strong's Concordance, the Greek word here for *divine* means "godlike" and the word *partakers* means "sharer" or "partaker." This scripture is saying that through these we may partake or share God's nature just like our children share our nature.

John 10:37-38 says, *"If I do not do the works of My Father, do not believe Me; but if I do, though you do not believe Me, believe the works, that you may know and believe that the Father is in Me, and I in Him."* Jesus, in this verse, is implying that the proof of sonship is in the ability to do what our Father does. Our DNA will always bleed through!

The five revelations in this chapter will help us to see ourselves from this new perspective. They will reveal how to live with a new awareness of our spirit – which will allow our spirit to direct and influence our lives and restore our hope and joy as we learn to live out of our new identity.

SUBSTANCE OF THE UNSEEN

"Then, the same day at evening, being the first day of the week,
when the doors were shut where the disciples were assembled,
for fear of the Jews, Jesus came and stood in the midst,
and said unto them, 'Peace be unto you.'"

John 20:19

Years ago, after reading John 20:19, God asked me if I knew how He entered the room where the disciples were hiding. Based on the ghost movies I had seen in the past, I had concluded that He could walk through walls because He had no substance. In my understanding, dead people were ghost-like and not as real or influential as people or things in this realm. Then I heard Him say, "No, I have more substance than the wall." The wall had less substance than He did; therefore, He could pass through it. When you think about it, the created cannot have more substance than the Creator. This may sound like an insignificant detail, but this revelation allowed me to begin placing more faith in the unseen realm because I began seeing God and His realm as having greater weight than my circumstances and things that were "seen" in this natural realm. I truly began to see this natural and visible realm as what will pass away, and His Spirit and our spirit as having the greater permanence and authority over the earth.

We are often taught to be fearful of acknowledging the spirit realm or of wanting to see the things of the spirit. Considering we are born of the Spirit, this seems like an odd teaching. I believe we need to cultivate an awareness of our spirit and the spirit realm. Many Christians think it is acceptable to talk about demons and the devil but not about angels and God's realm of the supernatural. It may be wise to be aware of the supernatural ways of satan, but remember that the ultimate supernatural being is God. How can we not study this aspect of Him, especially when He has commissioned us to walk in supernatural ways such as raising the dead, healing, and walking in the Spirit (Matthew 10:7-8)?

I like to think of my spirit as being somewhat like a water-soaked sponge. As I receive the substance of His presence through faith, my spirit expands and becomes weightier in the unseen realm. Since it takes up more space in the spirit realm when it is expanded, it has more influence and takes more ground; however, like a sponge, when it is dry, my spirit contracts, loses weight, and its influence lessens. When fear enters, this retraction happens, and we can literally feel our spirit contract and take up less space in order to protect itself.

When we are in the presence of God, the opposite is true. During an anointed time of worship, you have probably experienced your spirit expanding with courage and you began believing that you could do anything. Now that you are aware of what can happen in the presence of God, can I challenge you to intentionally become aware of when your spirit is expanding and when it is contracting? What are the thoughts that are affecting your spirit in each of these situations?

I read about a study on how confident people affect those around them in contrast to timid people. They first told a shy, timid person to enter a classroom very quietly and sit in the back row. When the shy, timid person did as he was instructed, hardly anyone turned around to see who had entered the room. Then they instructed a strong, confident person to do the same: enter the classroom very quietly and sit in the back row. When the strong, confident person entered, eighty percent of the class turned to see who had entered. The person of authority and confidence affected the room in a dramatic way. This leads me to believe that we are more aware of the spirits of people than we might think.

There are other examples of individuals unconsciously responding to people's spirits rather than to their physical presence. Have you ever felt someone watching you from behind? It is a strange feeling. When my daughter was a toddler, I used to be woken up in the middle of the night by her staring at me. Since I was in a deep sleep, my natural mind and senses were not alert; my daughter never even said anything that would prompt me to rise, but eventually, my spirit would wake me up because it was aware of her presence. Since our spirit is made in His image, it is not surprising that our spirit never sleeps and can become aware of other spirits in the room.

It is ironic how we as Christians are often times more aware of the demonic realm than the realm of the Kingdom. As a young Christian, I was very aware of the various spirits of fear or perversion present in a room. One of the places where I sensed this the most was in hotel rooms. On several occasions, I would walk into the room and have my feelings and emotions overwhelmed by the spiritual atmosphere in that room. My bad feelings and horrible dreams were a product of the negative spiritual residue, but what I didn't understand was that if there was substance to the demonic realm, then there had to be even greater substance to God's realm.

The truth that there is even greater substance to God's realm was brought home to me through an encounter I had many years ago. In this encounter, I was attempting to escape a room that felt oppressive and fearful because of an angry and bitter woman who was affecting the atmosphere. As I was leaving, I heard God quote 1 John 4:4, *"… He who is in you is greater than he who is in the world."* Immediately, this scripture went from a theology in my mind to a revelation in my heart. I saw that the Spirit of peace had more power to influence the atmosphere than any spirit of oppression or fear. When I walked back into the room, I felt myself clothed with the substance of His peace and love, and I could tell that His presence within me was changing the atmosphere.

This was a life-changing moment for me. I realized that in the past, I had faith in negative influences to affect people and atmospheres, but I had no grid for the power of love, peace, or joy to influence people or environments. If the substance of perversion could bring feelings of being slimed and dirty, then why couldn't the substance of holiness bring purity and love?

We can have a powerful influence on every environment that we enter. Have you ever been in a store or public place and suddenly felt tired, confused, or anxious? Often, we are picking up on a nearby person's spirit that is under that influence. In these situations, pay attention to your feelings and take note whether the condition remains after you leave. By doing this, you will learn to gauge the difference between oppression in an atmosphere and what is really going on in your spirit. The exciting point to all this is that we can do something about it. If people are really tuned in with each other's spirits and are subconsciously affected by them, then we can confidently and assertively walk in God's Spirit knowing that we are bringing peace, love, and joy into other people's lives.

Now I enjoy going to hotel rooms, where I not only cleanse it in the name of Jesus; but also leave the fragrance of heaven to woo people into His presence.

Being aware of the unseen realm and its ability to influence people and atmospheres is really just acknowledging that the kingdom of heaven is at hand and within our reach (Matthew 3:2). Everywhere we go we should consciously attach faith to our ability to bring the Kingdom of God.

APPLICATION

Train yourself to be more aware of your spirit by taking note of how you are affected in different venues. Instead of being a victim to the prevailing spirit, consciously picture yourself carrying the presence of God and emanating His grace, love, and peace. Watch and look for physical reactions to the presence you carry.

DECLARATION

The substance of God's love and peace
overwhelms people everywhere I go.

TRAIN
YOUR BRAIN

"For the hearts of this people have grown dull.
Their ears are hard of hearing. And their eyes they have closed,
lest they should see with their eyes and hear with their ears,
lest they should understand with their hearts and turn.
So that I should heal them."

Acts 28:27

While visiting an exhibit on the brain one day, God spoke to me about having eyes that see. One of the presentations had a computerized image of two seemingly identical portraits that were flipped upside down. The question below the pictures asked if they were indeed the same photo. I marked the "yes" box, and the computer flipped the portraits right side up. Instantly, it was obvious that one of the photos had been tweaked so that the nose, eye, or eyebrow had been moved out of place. They placed another set of upside-down portraits on the screen, and again, my brain could not distinguish any difference between the two; however, when they were placed right side up, I could see that again one of the faces had been altered.

Once I realized that one of the pictures would be altered every time, the computer showed me a new set of upside-down pictures. I began to train my brain not to rely on its first impression, but to actively search for tweaked areas in one of the pictures. Soon, while the pictures were upside down, I began to find the differences in them before they were turned upright. It was interesting to discover how often our brains do not see what reality is actually presenting. Our brains will interpret what it sees according to the filter of what it expects to see!

When I saw this exhibit, I was reminded of many verses in the Bible that make reference to having eyes that do not see. My thoughts were racing. I pondered the concept of the brain's ability to be trained as I just experienced in recognizing the differences between the two portraits. Could I also train my brain to see the unseen that was filtered out because of my brain's tendency to see only what it expects to see?

I realized that the first requirement for seeing altered areas of the portraits was to acknowledge that my brain was not always reliable in interpreting what it saw. I understood that I had to look with new eyes that were not filtered by the expected. I began to think of the many times my spirit tried to tell me something that my brain filtered out as not being reality, only to have it confirmed by other Christians as being true. For instance, I would sense a spiritual wind or hear that God wanted to touch depressed people, and then someone in the room would mention the exact same thing I heard or sensed. God was teaching my brain to trust the voice of my spirit.

Perhaps if we could train our brain to allow our spirit to see for us (rather than allowing the brain to be the only reliable source of sight), we could begin to walk in the Spirit like the Word says. Scripture mentions that we must take heed "how" we hear (Luke 8:18). We must train our brain to receive from the Spirit and allow ourselves to trust what our spirit is sensing, hearing, and seeing. We must lean on our spirit, which is a valuable sense that is as real as the other five senses we use.

The above referenced verse from Acts 28:27 talks about people who have eyes but do not see. Obviously, the context is not about blind people, but about people who cannot see the unseen realm. This scripture is talking about spiritual sight. It is important to realize that spiritual sight is not limited to a simple belief that there is a spiritual realm or to a belief in God. That is way too narrow a viewpoint. Unless we expect to see and hear from the unseen realm, then our experience will be limited to our limited expectations. In other words, our expectation will create the measure of our reception. Once we are able to admit that we have a spirit that is aware of and has knowledge about a realm that our brain cannot see or hear, then we will have made the first step in our journey of walking according to the spirit.

Often, I will ask my spirit what it is sensing or seeing in a room. In these situations, my brain is accustoming itself to using my spirit as another available source of information that it needs to factor into every day life. When we walk into a room, we should understand that our spirit has a better sense of our identity and capabilities than our intellect does. Our spirit knows that we cannot just talk people out of darkness. Our spirit is a powerful substance that becomes a force of light and revelation, so when we enter the room, we affect everyone around us. Our spirit opens a place for people to hear and receive truth that can set them free. Many people think the gifts of the Spirit, like prophecy and words of wisdom or knowledge, are random sovereign outbursts that God uses to speak to people. In reality, they are just a glimpse of what a normal Christian is capable of when using their spirit as a source of information.

I think one reason that many new Christians backslide is that we bring their spirit to life and then spend the rest of the time pretending that it does not exist. New believers are usually excited because, for the first time, they are aware of a new realm within them and around them. Their spirit is giving them glimpses of a whole new reality - the freeing power and joy of a new identity. They begin feeling empowered by what has been birthed within them.

Think about why some people become witches or warlocks. They have learned how to access the spirit realm and have resources beyond the natural realm. Unfortunately for them, they become slaves and tools to a tormenting taskmaster, the devil, because they are accessing the spirit realm illegally. As believers, we have legal access in the spirit realm and in heavenly places. In fact, Ephesians 2 says we are actually seated in heavenly places, which is referring to the unseen realm of the Kingdom of God. His realities and divine nature are now available for us to use in this present world. If new believers are not taught to walk and see by the spirit, they will revert to living according to old natural means. Believers are unconsciously looking for places that make them feel alive, or places that bring awareness to the fact that they are more spirit than flesh.

My passion is to stir passionless Christians who know something is wrong and unfulfilling in their life, but do not have the answers of what is missing. I do not claim to have all those answers, but I do know that when I am allowing God to nourish my spirit and am learning to actually live spiritually, then life becomes an exhilarating adventure of walking according to His empowering supernatural gifts and resources.

APPLICATION

Consider an area of your life that has become boring or passionless. Ask God what that area should look like once impacted by the supernatural. Then, allow God to set you back on the journey of learning to walk according to the spirit.

DECLARATION

My spirit is arising within me.
I can feel it and hear it.

three

HEARING FROM OUR SPIRIT

*"God is Spirit, and those who worship Him
must **worship in spirit** and truth."*

John 4:24

*"When Jesus **perceived in His spirit** that they reasoned thus within
themselves, He said to them, 'Why do you reason about these things in
your hearts?'"*

Mark 2:8

The process of learning to distinguish between the voice of our
spirit and the voice of our mind is a journey of trial and error. Many
Christians struggle to discern His voice because they have faulty
beliefs which actually hinder their ability to hear. In order to relax
and begin to hear God, we need to establish two basic beliefs that
will facilitate the process.

The first belief that facilitates the process of discerning the voice of our spirit from the voice of our mind is the belief that God is okay with process. In fact, He is the originator of it. For instance, when the Israelites needed a Savior, God did not send a man, He sent a baby. Men and women are not born adults, they are born as babies unable to take care of themselves. Through practice, they learn to walk, talk, and develop great skills. He uses seeds that, in due process, bring forth mature fruit.

Just as we encourage and celebrate the process that babies go through to reach maturity, God encourages and celebrates our baby steps of learning to walk and communicate with Him. In my journey to understand and mature in my spiritual new birth, God told me to stop seeing myself as a failure and to see myself as being in process. When we are attempting to understand the voice of the Spirit, we may make mistakes, but God does not call our mistakes "failures," He calls them "learning!" No one calls a toddler a failure when he falls down or cannot speak as clearly as an adult; yet, we often do not give Christians or ourselves the same grace while maturing as a spiritual being.

The second belief that helps us to differentiate the voice of our spirit from the voice of our mind is two-fold. First, we need to fully believe that God can compensate for our apparent spiritual deafness. Second, we need to believe that He is able to cover us when we hear incorrectly. Taking hold of these two beliefs will help take the fear of making a mistake out of the equation. Fear actually creates static in the spirit realm that prevents us from hearing God's voice clearly. We remove the fear of making a mistake by making our God bigger than any mistake we can make. Yes, we need to get counsel and line up what we hear with the written Word of God, but once we have done that, we just need to believe that if we are wrong, God can cover us if we have misheard.

With these beliefs firmly established, we can move on to the actual process of increasing our ability to hear the spirit within. It is important to note that many people expect God's voice to sound completely different than any voice they have heard before. Because of this, they do not recognize when He is speaking. Sometimes believers mistake the enemy's voice for their own, and are surprised to find that God's voice can also be confused with their own. "When God speaks, it's not always a huge spectacle, but He usually speaks in the still small voice (1 Kings 19:11-13). Through practice and knowing what to look for, we can become confident in our ability to hear His voice.

Once we believe that our spirit (which is one with the Holy Spirit) has the ability to impart wisdom, knowledge, and an awareness of what is happening in the unseen realm, we should have an expectation that our spirit has something to say as often as any other sense (like touch or smell) has information to communicate.

When I told God that I wanted to learn how to discern and hear the voice of my spirit, He actually began an interesting and specific process in me. One day, I had a thought flash through my mind that I should take a dessert to a certain meeting. I dismissed the thought because I knew someone else had been contacted to bring dessert. When I arrived, I discovered that she was not able to come or bring dessert. Strangely enough, in a short amount of time, a few other things of this nature began happening. I began to realize that my spirit may have more information than my brain, so I started to take heed of those flashes of information.

On another occasion, while I was in a prayer meeting, I had a thought flash through my mind that there was a large angel standing behind me. At first, I was able to believe that this was my spirit giving me cool information, but then another thought came. This time, it flashed through my mind much the same way, but I heard that the angel had red hair. This information (an angel with red hair) was so bizarre that doubts assailed me. Even though I received the information the same way, I had a different response. My brain rationalized that surely my overly active imagination was making this up! Instead of leaning into the impression and asking more questions, I shut down the voice I was hearing in my mind and relied on my own understanding. However, after the prayer meeting, a person came to me and said they had seen a big angel behind me with red hair! Wow, that really raised my faith in my ability to hear. As the voice of the Spirit continued to speak, I realized that I was improving my ability to hear and distinguish what was of the Spirit and what was not.

None of these examples I shared were life or death situations, but the practice of hearing with outside confirmation on the small things has helped me to trust in the bigger things I hear now. Learning to hear when there is no crisis is good practice for when we are under fire and need urgent help. I have discovered that the Spirit loves to teach, so I enjoy asking questions and dialoguing about things that have no major consequence. My goal is to trust what my spirit is saying as equally as I trust my natural sight, hearing, smell, or touch. This will enable me to live with the conscious reality that I am living not just in this natural realm, but also in the realm of the spirit (which is not limited to my natural mind).

APPLICATION

By faith, ask your spirit questions like "Where are the angels standing in this room?" Before your day or week begins, listen for thoughts that will apply to your day or week, and write them down to compare with how the actual day or week plays out. Ask God to teach you to hear more clearly and expect some fun. He is not a harsh teacher; He likes to have fun during the process!

DECLARATION

My brain hears and responds easily to the voice of the Spirit.

four

OUR SUPERNATURAL IDENTITY

"By which have been given to us exceedingly great and precious promises, that through these you may be partakers of the divine nature."

2 Peter 1:4

"For those who live according to the flesh set their minds on the things of the flesh, but those who live according to the Spirit, the things of the Spirit."

Romans 8:5

Many Christians are still struggling with their identity because they are looking at what they do to determine who they are. I like to remind people that when an unsaved person who has not been born again does a righteous act, it does not make them a righteous person. Their DNA is still that of a sinner. Even so, it follows that when a saint or righteous person sins, it does not make them a sinner. They are a righteous person doing a sinful act. Their DNA is still that of a righteous person. The unseen force of our beliefs is more powerful than most people realize. A favorite quote of mine is from one of my pastors, Kris Vallotton. Kris says, "If you believe you are a sinner, you will sin by faith."

One reason many struggle to act righteous is because they are trying to do what they don't believe they *are*. It is vital for us to change how we think in order to have a lasting change in our actions. According to Romans 12:2, we are transformed not by trying harder to change, but by renewing our mind. If we want our character, lifestyle or heart to be transformed, we must think differently than we now think. We will not be able to consistently and easily act righteous until we believe we *are* righteous.

Too many believers try to determine their identity from their past failures or experiences rather than from their new birth. What would happen if a baby established its identity from its past rather than from its parents? The baby would think it did not have the "gift of walking," the "gift of talking," etc. But we know that babies watch their parents, not their past, to determine what they are capable of learning to accomplish. We are born again spirits, and it is time to realize that when Romans 8:5 talks about living *"according to the Spirit"* by setting our minds on the *"things of the Spirit,"* it is an analogy of *how* one learns to live. We must be like newborn babies and focus on Christ and the Father to determine our potential. We should walk with the core value of a baby, which is: I may not be able to do that yet, but I am made in God's image; therefore, I have all the potential within my DNA to do what He is doing. This gives new meaning to John 5:19 where Jesus says He only *does* what He *sees the Father do*.

Remember that in the Greek, the word "repent" really means to *change the way we think*. If we narrow repentance down to only mean that we are sorry for something, then we will have repented enough for forgiveness but not enough for transformation. Do not just repent from sin – repent to transformation. One day, I was crying out for God to "take my heart" because I thought my sin issue was a heart issue. I thought that if I could just give God more of my heart, then my character would finally be transformed. As I was crying and begging Him to take more of my heart, He interrupted me by saying, "Wendy, I have your heart; I need your mind." It was then that He began taking me on a journey of renewing my mind as the pathway of transformation.

If you feel hopeless about yourself and have spent years trying to change, then I want to remind you that the definition of insanity is doing the same thing over and over and expecting different results. I challenge you to begin changing what you believe about yourself and who you believe you are. Don't be satisfied with just a mental assent, but cultivate a deep belief change that results in an emotional shift regarding who you are.

Henry David Thoreau once said, "As a single footstep will not make a path on the earth, so a single thought will not make a pathway in the mind. To make a deep physical path, we walk again and again. To make a deep mental path, we must think over and over the kind of thoughts we wish to dominate our lives."

APPLICATION

Write down some new identity declarations that line up with your new birth status. As you do this, consider whom your Daddy really is and ask what He is able to do?

DECLARATION

I am a partaker of the divine nature, and I look like my Father.

ACCESSING
THE KINGDOM

"The time is fulfilled, and the kingdom of God is at hand.
Repent, and believe in the gospel."

Mark 1:15

Another way of saying the last part of this scripture is "change the way you think so you can believe in the good news." Without major mind shifts led by the Spirit of God, we will not be able to fully comprehend what absolute good news it is to finally have the kingdom at hand for us to access.

While reading Matthew 28:18-19 (*"All authority has been given to Me in heaven and on earth. Go therefore and make disciples of all the nations..."*), I heard God say to me that Christians tend to think that making disciples is making people look and act like Jesus. Then He explained that to really be a disciple, we must *believe* like Jesus. What is the difference? Well, if we try to get people to act *like* Jesus, they will be trying to "act" like something they do not believe they are – it will just be a performance. This makes the Christian life very difficult. But if we *believe* like Jesus, we will know we are beloved children of God, in right standing, wholly accepted and heard by the Father. It will cause us to believe that power, healing, love, wisdom, and righteousness is something we are – not something we do. When disciples have the same beliefs as Jesus, they will effortlessly live out of their identity. They will no longer need to work for love, rather they will work from love.

That is why my husband and I tell people everywhere we go that the prayer of the hour is not, "Jesus, tell me what to do," but "Jesus, tell me what to believe." Mark 1:15 does not say, "Repent, and do," it says, "Repent, and believe." I discovered that often what I thought I believed was only a mental assent. To turn something from a mental assent to a belief takes time and effort.

God told me I would know if I really believed a truth when my emotions lined up with what I believed. *When a truth becomes a part of the spirit of our mind (our unconscious thought patterns), then it is a true belief.* For example, when we first learn a new skill, like driving, we do it consciously and have to think carefully. But after years of driving, most of our actions and reactions are unconscious. The same pattern applies with faith. For instance, if we have a deep unconscious belief that God is good and that all things work out for our good, then even when circumstances seem to be at odds with that belief, our first reaction will be to look for the blessing that is coming. We will not imagine it getting worse, but we will be looking for the answer. We will not have unconscious expectations that the rug is about to be pulled out from under us or that good things cannot last. Instead, we will believe that God will take us from glory to glory because He is the God of increase. In other words, we will be anticipating more good!

We are able to drive a car with unconscious precision now because we first taught our brain on purpose. We trained it how to react in certain circumstances like stopping at a light and putting our turn signal on. I believe that Philippians 4:8 tells us a secret to living in the Spirit. It says, *"Think on these things."* In other words, we are to think on purpose. Think, speak, declare, and imagine on purpose until it becomes a part of who you are. *As we think, speak, declare and imagine "whatever is of good report," we will begin to experience what we are declaring without conscious effort. The goal is for our actions to come from the spirit of our mind* (Ephesians 4:23).

I remember a transforming moment when I was fully aware that a mental assent became a core belief. My husband and I were traveling in a car and making declarations together. One of our declarations is that we will have favor with God and man everywhere we go. We enjoy trying new things, so on the spur of the moment I added to the declaration, "Even if we try to make people dislike us, we couldn't." As soon as the words left my mouth, I felt something in my mind shift. A real revelation hit me – when we carry the substance of favor, we no longer have to perform for people to like us! From that moment on, I not only had a mental assent, but I also added something to the spirit of my mind!

Before this revelation, I constantly had to remind myself that I needed to relax and not perform for people. Once the belief solidified that a spirit of favor was upon me, I noticed that I rarely had to consciously relax and try to be myself. Who I am became enough, and I was freed to be me all the time.

As you renew your mind and think on purpose, remember that it is a process. It is important not to condemn yourself during the process of transition from mental assent to belief. Condemnation and fear of displeasing God actually hinders the work in progress. God created our mind to accept what it hears over and over – *"Faith comes by hearing"* (Romans 10:17). Relax and think and speak on purpose!

APPLICATION

Do you anticipate failure or believe that good cannot last? Are you afraid that if people really knew you, they would not think as well of you? Do you think you will never get out of debt or that God could never make you a blazing success? Ask God for a revelation of an area of your unconscious thought life that does not match up with His truth that the Kingdom is within you. Then, ask God for His truth in that area.

DECLARATION

I anticipate good coming my way.
Goodness and mercy follow me all the days of my life.

LIMITLESS RECEPTION

The next section of revelations is my favorite. For many years, I attempted to get results in my Christian life by trying to do things differently or better. When results did not improve, I believed that either I was unworthy, a failure, unready, or the enemy was hindering the process. Section two reveals that there is a whole other option of why things are not changing! It is our perception or view of truth that is putting limits on our ability to receive.

Deception distorts perception, and distorted perception limits our reception! The problem with deception is that we do not know we are deceived. It is an unconscious belief or conclusion we have built in our mind that was based on faulty information or past experience.

For instance, as a young Christian I heard many testimonies about the devil's ability to attack, especially when one is doing something for God. Now I know these people were trying to testify that God was faithful, but what I concluded was that anytime I am doing something for God, I would be assaulted. My faith was not attached to God's faithfulness, but in satan's ability to attack! This perception of the normal Christian life created a lifestyle of having unnecessary spiritual attacks. I was actually limiting my ability to receive protection because I believed that attack was right and normal.

God asked my husband and I a great question: "Why do you have more faith in the enemy's ability to attack, than in My ability to protect?" This challenged our patterns of thinking, and we immediately repented and realized that we are not the attacked ones, but the attackers! We get to go on the offensive. We should talk often about God's protection, not satan's attacks, because whatever we spend time talking about, we will see more of that manifest in our lives.

Perceptions can be changed. The best way to know whether you are under deception is to look at the fruit produced by what you are believing. Does it bring hopelessness, fear, or condemnation? If it does, then it isn't from God. The good news of the Kingdom will always bring hope, empowerment, and peace. We have inherited a victorious gospel – not just a "survive and cope" gospel.

I pray the following revelations will radically change your life as they have mine. I cannot express how many things changed in my life simply because I chose to form new perceptions about God, myself, and others.

THE POWER
OF A BLESSING

"Then Isaac trembled exceedingly, and said, 'Who?
Where is the one who hunted game and brought it to me?
I ate all of it before you came, and I have blessed him—and
indeed he shall be blessed.' When Esau heard the words of his father,
he cried with an exceedingly great and bitter cry,
and said to his father, 'Bless me—me also, O my father!'"

Genesis 27:33-34

In the 1980's, it seemed the church was very aware of the demonic influence in the world. We were taught to avoid anything that might have an evil origin or could be attached to a curse. I don't have a problem with this teaching, but it never seemed to be balanced out with the power of God. God reminded me of a time, in the 1990's, when some witches went to a church in California, cursed it, and drew an evil design on the back wall. The Christians in our region gathered together to pray and break off any consequence of that curse. That may have been a good decision, but we were giving that curse so much attention. Every Sunday at that very church, the pastor would release a blessing over the congregation as it dismissed. When God reminded me of that event, He asked me, "Why do you have more expectation from a witch's curse than from a pastor's blessing?" That question rocked me! I had to admit that my expectation from a blessing was woefully small – if existent at all. My thinking had to change.

Why has the church taught people to have a huge expectation or fear of a witch's curse, yet failed to teach and demonstrate the power of the Christian's blessing? It seems to me that we have unwittingly been teaching the church only how to play defense. But every great coach knows that you only win games because you have both a strong defense and a strong offense. When we play offense, we are in possession of the "ball" (the keys of the kingdom). We get to go on the attack. If we believe that a person under the influence of the demonic can do mighty supernatural things, then why are we so hesitant to believe that as partakers of the divine nature, we also can do supernatural works?

My pastor, Bill Johnson, once shared about the superiority of New Testament living. In the Old Testament, when an Israelite touched a leper or the dead, he became unclean; however, in the New Testament, when Jesus touched a leper, the leper became clean – and when he got near the dead, they became alive! This radically transformed my perception! It helped me to see that Christ changed the equation. The curses have been overcome by the blessings. Many are still living an Old Testament experience even though **we are equipped through the cross to bring life and healing everywhere the curse has brought death and destruction.**

Even in the Old Testament, God's people had a high value for the power of a blessing. They knew it was irrevocable and powerfully affected the future. Our false concept of humility has birthed a multitude of powerless Christians who don't think they have a right or mandate to place blessings upon their families, cities, and nations. We are walking into a new season, where we must recognize that we have a great responsibility for passing a blessing to our children's children.

In Ephesians 1:3, we are told that we have been blessed with every spiritual blessing. I do not believe the Church has even begun to tap into the fullness of this scripture! What does being blessed with every spiritual blessing mean or look like? Many people can picture what a curse might look like, but few can picture what a blessing looks like. Witches are usually very specific about how a curse will affect a person. As Christians, we need to be more specific about what the effects of a blessing will be when we declare it.

In the Old Testament, people could actually recognize blessings on people or tribes. Obed-Edom in 2 Samuel 6:11,12 is a great example. In this story, the people reported to King David that Obed-Edom and all his house were being blessed because the ark of God was residing there. Is it not logical that unsaved people today should recognize that we are blessed because He resides in our house?

I was taught that when a person is under a curse, he can do all the right things and bad will still happen. If that is true, then if we are blessed, could we do things wrong and still have good happen? I am not suggesting that we do wrong things on purpose, but believing in the power of a blessing will greatly reduce the anxiety of perfectionism.

My husband and I had such a radical perception shift in regards to the power of a blessing that we started to fake sneeze because people would say, "Bless you." It was fun and may seem a little silly, but we were trying to develop a greater value for blessings. In Genesis 27, Jacob realized the power of a blessing to the point that he was willing to deceive his father.

Many people talk about cities held under the power of a curse, but it is time to experience cities held under the power of a blessing! If sinful people create curses in a region by constant immoral or evil actions, then we must also believe that we create strongholds of blessing in regions through worship, kind acts, or taking communion by faith. Everything we do should seed the atmosphere with blessing upon blessing.

Proverbs 11:11 says, *"By the blessing of the upright the city is exalted, but it is overthrown by the mouth of the wicked."* If we really believed that our city is exalted by our blessing, then perhaps we would spend more time speaking a blessing over it. And if it works for a city, might it not work for an individual or work place?

APPLICATION

Take time to imagine the consequences of the power of a blessing. Make a list of people or places that you want to bless and proclaim specific blessings like success, peace, favor or joy over them.

DECLARATION

I bless my descendants with wisdom, love, prosperity, and peace in every area of their life.

THE POWER
OF LIGHT

*"You are of God, little children, and have overcome them:
because greater is He that is in you, than he who is in the world."*

1 John 4:4

There are many stories throughout the New Testament where a battle
between good and evil is presented. In Acts 19, there is a story about
a man possessed by an evil spirit who leapt on the seven sons of Sceva
and overpowered them, sending them fleeing naked and wounded.
Another story is found in Mark 5. It describes a man possessed
by a legion of demons that no man could tame, or chains could
hold. In the past when I read these stories, I used to focus on how
powerful the spirits of darkness were which influenced people to do
supernatural acts. But then a new thought struck me: "If one man
under the influence of evil spirits can do that much, then what are the
possibilities of a man under the influence of the Holy Spirit?" If evil
spirits can overcome seven men and break chains, then perhaps we

have vastly underestimated the capabilities of believing Christians. I think we mistakenly tend to possess a greater understanding of what a demon-possessed man can do than what a Holy Spirit-filled Christian can do.

Most of us believe that opening spiritual doors can give the enemy legal access to a person, causing them to not only do things they never desired before, but also causing them to do super-human acts of strength and break laws of nature (such as body contortions, levitation, and so on). Christians often hold these beliefs to be true, yet most people seem to think that when we open the spiritual door to the Holy Spirit, He is unable to change our desires or enable us to do supernatural acts. I believe that under His influence we should be able to do greater things than Jesus did (John 14:12). Walking on water, being translated, and having visions should be part of the normal Christian life. Instead, we limit the working of His authority and power through us because of wrong doctrine, unworthiness, false humility, and the fear of making mistakes.

It is time to arise, shine, and let His light devour darkness and the works of the enemy. Often we think being powerful is only for leaders or perfect people. Although leading people requires character and a proven lifestyle of overcoming, having authority over darkness is inherently given when we become born again and receive revelation of our position as light. I have heard of people operating in powerful gifts on the first day of their salvation, so do not underestimate the power within you to work in supernatural ways. If you are waiting for some invisible measurement of qualification, then you will probably wait a long time. The only qualification is faith!

When Jesus says we are the light of the world (Matthew 5:14), the word *light* means "to shine" or "make manifest." This is not just a cute saying or theological thought, but something to be experienced. Our presence should make the kingdom of God visibly manifest in the world. I am not referring to just God's character or holiness – it is bigger than that. It is also our given authority to take dominion and restore all of creation into proper order and health.

I believe the concept of Christians being light is not just a symbolic thought. I believe the light we contain is an actual substance that affects the atmosphere, our lives, and the spiritual realm. This light can be seen in various degrees according to the faith and understanding of the one carrying it. In other words, the measure of weight and authority that our light carries will be based on the measure of our belief that we carry this substance and understand its power and impact.

I once had an experience where I saw this power manifest before my eyes. A woman came to me for some issues in her life that needed wisdom and inner healing. The counseling time was not getting anywhere and she could not seem to understand the truths I was attempting to share with her. I felt God say I was to pray for her. As I began to pray, I heard myself saying, "Light, more light, light," over and over. I sensed the light of God hovering over us. She began to cry and receive God's truth and answers for what was troubling her. A powerful transformation happened for her that day.

When the church understands the power of the light within them, it will transform everything! We will not just trust in our words to get people saved, but we will trust the light within us to remove blindness from people so that when we speak, bolts of revelation will lead to extraordinary salvations. People will be drawn to our light and follow us around, wanting what we have. Confusion will be restored to order and no one in our presence will be depressed.

We know the Holy Spirit is not living in us because He needs a place to live. He lives in us because He wants fellowship with us and He desires to manifest the power of the Kingdom through us. In John 20:21, Jesus said, *"As the Father sent Me, I also send you."* He was sent to destroy the works of the devil – the things that torment, bind, and blind people. He was also equipped with an anointing that heals, delivers, and brings revelation. In the same way, we are also sent. We are the light of this world, and we need to arise and shine (Matthew 5:14 and Isaiah 60:1). Go in the power of this revelation!

APPLICATION

Meditate on what life looks like when you are clothed in a light that causes darkness to flee. Picture it overcoming sickness, blind eyes, hopelessness, and despair.

DECLARATION

The light of God dwells in me
and destroys the works of the enemy.

three

LEARNING TO RECEIVE

Part One

*"The people who know their God shall be strong,
and carry out great exploits."*

Daniel 11:32b

Our perception of God will affect our reception from Him. For many years, I only saw God as my Master; therefore, my reception from Him was limited to hearing Him tell me what to do or hearing rebukes for not doing something correctly. During that time, I lost not only the ability to dream, but I also lost any concept of my own identity. Even though I had been uniquely made with love, I thought God wanted me to symbolically disappear and become just an obedient slave. Slaves do not dream about the future because they are in bondage to someone else's dream. I was thinking I was a slave to God instead of His friend. When we perceive God only as Master, it will prevent us from receiving all the love songs He sings over us (Zephaniah 3:17). It will also prevent us from walking in His delegated authority to use the gifts of His Spirit. On the other hand, when we receive Him as our Father, a new world opens up for us.

As we begin to realize the God of the universe is our Father, we will be able to receive from Him, not just as a wealthy philanthropist, but as our loving, caring, and giving Dad. A philanthropist gives an occasional handout, but a good Dad gives constant nourishment to the body, soul, and spirit. The Father takes responsibility for every aspect of His children.

God is the perfect Father. He gives identity, love, and training so we may prosper in all things. I am enjoying my Christian life so much more ever since I enlarged my perception of who God is to me. Now, I am learning to laugh, dream, and receive blessings and encouragement from Him. I can relate to Him as a beloved daughter and receive things from Him that I didn't earn through performance, but received through relationship.

Another perception that hindered my receiving was based on the religious belief that God holds back blessings of success, anointing, and finances until we have proven ourselves as faithful or worthy enough. Because of this belief, I was unable to stand in faith for anything that took me beyond my current experience in life. I lived from miracle to miracle rather than in the constant blessing of God. I unconsciously kept my success at my perceived level of worth or value. Since the view of my worth and value were distorted, I was never able to move into the full destiny of my calling. When we seem to become stuck at a certain level of breakthrough, it is not usually because we are doing something wrong – it is often a belief issue.

For many years, I perceived God as the One who forgives but not as the One who empowers. I was constantly begging for forgiveness because I did not know He could empower me to change. If you are struggling with receiving the empowerment of His Spirit and think He is holding out on you for some reason, I suggest you read John 20:21-22, where Jesus breathed on the disciples and said, "As the Father sent Me, I also send you. Receive the Holy Spirit." This means since the Father sent Jesus, who was fully empowered with the resources of Heaven, so also Jesus sends us with the same empowerment. We must understand that He desires to empower His people.

We often make receiving more difficult than it should be. Matthew 10:8 says, *"Heal the sick, cleanse the lepers, raise the dead, cast out demons. Freely you have received, freely give."* I read that verse a thousand times, but it didn't seem to be manifesting in my life. I found myself constantly begging for His anointing. One day, Jesus interrupted my prayer by telling me it wasn't that hard to receive the anointing. This confused me until He added, "Even a handkerchief can do it!" He reminded me of Acts 19:11-12 when aprons and handkerchiefs soaked up Paul's anointing to heal the sick and deliver people from evil spirits. If a handkerchief can *"heal the sick, cleanse the lepers, raise the dead, and cast out demons"* (Matthew 10:8), then surely we can!

Since this revelation, when I am in His presence, I often pretend to be a handkerchief and soak up His anointing. While soaking, I like to think about the effects of a person being out in the sun. We may not feel as if anything is happening, but within a few hours, the manifestation of a tan or sunburn will be evident. With this in mind, I remind myself that it is impossible to be in His presence and not be changed!

There are so many more aspects of God to receive than we are currently experiencing. What would the Body of Christ look like if we were to perceive Him correctly? First John 3:2 says, "When we see Him we will be like Him." That process begins here on earth, not just in heaven. Every new revelation of Him transforms us and enables us to attempt exploits that go beyond our natural abilities and talents.

Let me challenge you with these question: Why are many believers not walking in the fullness we're called to? Is it because God is holding out on us? Or is our perception limiting our reception?

APPLICATION

Spend some time waiting in God's presence. Pretend to be a handkerchief and soak up His love and anointing. *For more information on soaking, see our website* www.ignitinghope. com *for free downloads or articles.*

DECLARATION

I easily rest and receive in His presence.

Limitless Reflection
four

LEARNING
TO RECEIVE
Part Two

*"He who receives a prophet in the name of a prophet shall
receive a prophet's reward. And he who receives a righteous man in the
name of a righteous man shall receive a righteous man's reward."*

Matthew 10:41

Our negative perceptions will not only limit our reception from God, but will also restrict our ability to receive from other people. In Mark 6, Jesus could do no mighty miracles in His hometown because their perception of Him was based on His past history with them. To them, He was just the carpenter's son. Therefore, all they could receive from Him was carpentry work.

It is important that we perceive people correctly. I love 2 Corinthians 5:16, which says, *"We regard no one according to the flesh."* I wonder how many times I have failed to receive a blessing or miracle because my perception of a person limited my ability to receive what they carried? I am struck by the thought that God's idea of who is worthy to flow in the supernatural is much different from mine.

I find it interesting that we are able to fail in some areas of life, while at the same time, succeed in others. This is because revelation and victory can touch one part of our life while we are still learning in others. I may have an area of victory that can help you, even though I am still experiencing defeat in a different area. In this reality, there is a caution that we need to pay attention to. If someone is experiencing defeat in areas that I am strong in, I can be quick to jump to the conclusion that, if they can't do what I can do, then they are weaker than me in every area of life. If I do that, then I am limiting what I can receive from them.

There was a lady in a church who didn't want a certain person who had anger issues to pray for her. I knew this person with anger issues had a huge healing anointing, so I encouraged the other lady to receive prayer for migraines from her. After much indecision, she reluctantly agreed. As she received prayer, she fell under the power of God and was healed. The person who did in fact struggle with anger was still anointed, so when the sick lady opened up to her and was unoffended, she was healed because she was now able to receive from her.

Religious people tend to be offended when God uses imperfect people, but that is all He has to work with! Flowing in the supernatural is a DNA issue, not a performance issue. Humans can walk, talk, and think because it is in their DNA, not because they earned the privilege. It is the same principle for walking in supernatural gifts. *(Please take note that leadership positions and places of authority should not be given simply because someone flows in the supernatural, but because they have exhibited the ability to live a victorious lifestyle based on their revelation of the promises of God.)*

When we learn to receive from imperfect people, it enables us to benefit from their strengths and to honor them for their talents, even while they are still in process. If we are fear based, we will be too afraid of the power of their weaknesses to receive anything from them. Instead of living in fear, we should strive to be faith based, believing that our strengths and giftings will benefit and influence others, while we are being influenced by the strengths of others.

I used to believe that if I honored people for their strengths while they still had issues, they would think I was approving of everything in their lives. This is not true. I found that as I acknowledged the gold in people, they were actually more willing to work on their unresolved issues. It is not always our responsibility to "fix people," but we can love them through it. As a leader, you can only lead those you love.

For ten years, we pastored in a gold mining community. The gold mine had modern methods that made mining for microscopic gold actually worthwhile. They had huge dump trucks as tall as houses, which moved tons of dirt every day. Even though a lot of dirt was moved, the focus was always on the gold. As we pastored that church, we used the same method; no matter how much dirt we moved, the people always knew our focus was on the gold. We only moved dirt because we saw gold in the people.

Let's celebrate the gold in people and receive the gift that is within them. Soon they will be asking for help to remove the dirt so more gold can be discovered!

APPLICATION

Think of a person in your life that you struggle with personally. Start a list of their good qualities and gifts. Ponder how you may honor and receive the gifts that are in them.

DECLARATION

I see and draw out the gold in people.

third reflection

ABUNDANT
LIVING

T his third section is based on my reflections on how to live the abundant life Jesus promises. The question of the hour is this: "Do I lower my standard of what an abundant life looks like to fit my experience, or do I raise it to fit *according to His riches in glory?*" (Philippians 4:19, Ephesians 1:18).

One of the greatest revelations of this generation is the understanding that the Kingdom of Heaven is a present tense reality for all believers. It is at hand and within reach. In fact, we are already living in His Kingdom, but we are unable to fully see or access it because of our under-developed ability to see and hear by the Spirit.

Matthew 10:7-8 says, *"And as you go, preach, saying, 'The kingdom of heaven is at hand.' Heal the sick, cleanse the lepers, raise the dead, cast out demons. Freely you have received, freely give."*

The kingdom mentioned in these verses is accessed by faith and revelation of the Word of God. In this kingdom we are beloved sons and daughters of the King. We are partakers of the divine nature, given delegated dominion in this present age over darkness, sickness, death, and the earth. This is what Jesus meant when He said He came to give us an abundant life (John 10:10).

For most of my Christian life, I thought we were not seeing the manifestation of these truths because we were unworthy. While I lived under this assumption, hardly anything changed. Then I had a revelation of Romans 12:2, which implies that if I want to be transformed to manifest the divine nature, I need to renew my mind. I need to change the way I think! I began to realize that changing my thinking enables me to "see" things differently. Renewing my mind helps me to see the unseen laws of the Spirit, the substance of the Kingdom, the angelic, and even my true identity, as never before.

This new revelation set me free to not just "endure" life, but to be an overcomer. Once I could see myself and the world through the eyes of the Spirit and the Word, I realized we are not victims to this world, or God's supposed capriciousness, but our lives are directed by our own beliefs and views of ourselves.

Luke 8:16-18 says, *"No one, when he has lit a lamp, covers it with a vessel or puts it under a bed, but sets it on a lampstand, that those who enter may see the light. For nothing is secret that will not be revealed, nor anything hidden that will not be known and come to light. Therefore take heed how you hear."*

I used to think these verses were about me not hiding my light and a warning that all my sins would be revealed, therefore I better not be involved with evil or unworthy things; however, when these verses are read in their correct context, they are really saying that God will not hide His light and mysteries of the Kingdom from us if we will take heed how we hear.

First Corinthians 2:12 says we have received the Spirit so *"We might know the things that have been freely given to us by God."* For us to learn *how* to hear, we must be able to discern the voice of the Spirit. To learn *what* to hear, as mentioned in Mark 4:24, we must filter our hearing through the promises of God and His Word and not through our past experiences, religious teachings, or unrenewed mind.

These next five reflections describe the supernatural laws of the spirit and heavenly resources that were created for our benefit. I pray that through these thoughts you will know the things freely given to you by God.

LIFE
MORE ABUNDANT

*"Woe to you lawyers! For you have taken away the key of knowledge.
You did not enter in yourselves,
and those who were entering in you hindered."*

Luke 11:52

Many religious teachers have narrowed down the Christian life to kneeling at the cross or to a continual dying to self. The Christian life was never supposed to be about dying; it was meant to be about living. The cross was not the goal; it was the method or means to the goal. Jesus didn't die on the cross so you could die. He died so you could live! God desires us to live a resurrected life in accordance with the original intent before Adam sinned. We do not glorify God in our dying but in our living!

Jesus says in John 10:10, *"The thief does not come except to steal, and to kill, and to destroy. **I have come** that they may have **life**, and that they may have it more **abundantly**."* In this passage, Jesus is talking about life on planet earth, not just in heaven. Even more amazing, He is talking to people who are already alive and breathing.

Is it possible that life is more than survival, performance, or whatever we have narrowed it down to in order to feel like we are successfully living? I think it is.

We become brokers of death when all we have to offer is rules for living without a supernatural means to attain it. In Luke 11:44 we read, *"For you are like graves which are not seen."* Jesus spoke this to the Pharisees who were making themselves look good on the outside but were neglecting their inner life. When we think that life is only about character, service, obedience, and rules and neglect our spirit, we become like the Pharisees in Luke 11. When we are like graves that are not seen, we may seem to be alive to the natural eye, but we are really only a receptacle of death. In Matthew 23:27, Jesus called the religious leaders of His day white washed tombs. What is in a tomb? It is a place where spiritless bodies dwell. In other words, He accused the leaders of having no spirit.

Let me ask you this – Are you spending more time trying "not" to do things, or are you focused on releasing the divine nature that is within you? Good character is not synonymous with "walking in the Spirit" – it is a *fruit* of walking in the Spirit. Instead of focusing on dying to self, try thinking about what makes you come alive.

For many years, my life was all about containment and control – dying to self. I rarely offered my opinion unless someone insisted, and I certainly never did anything that would draw attention to me! My life, my voice, and my actions were always contained so I could fit in anywhere and be accepted. Because of this, I became nothing and did not attempt anything that might cause failure. I thought success was never failing. I certainly was not attaining the abundant life with this mindset!

I was also experiencing nightmares on a regular basis about

demonic beings coming at me. I was unable to rebuke them because they would cause me to be mute. I would try and try to speak to them in the name of Jesus, but the words would actually get caught in my throat and begin to choke me! I did not realize these were more than just nightmares. They were an expression of how I was living my life.

Little by little, God helped release me from my self-containment. I learned to lift my hands in worship, dance with joy, pray out loud, and try new things. With every new outward action, a little more of me was being released. But the biggest breakthrough came one day in a worship service. I heard God say quite clearly, **"Give My Spirit a voice!"** I had not realized that in my attempt to be dignified and contained, I was also constricting the Holy Spirit within me. As soon as He spoke these words, something broke loose. In my desire to be invisible, I made Him invisible! My shyness, fear of attention, and control was not my personality; it was the enemy taking away my voice and the ability to reveal Jesus through me. I broke off the spirit of muteness and decided to give Him my voice.

Before this experience, I only focused on dying to self. Afterward, He began to teach me how to come alive. As a result, my passion for Him increased, hope was restored, and life began to flow. After so many years of trying to be nothing, I realized I did not even know who or what I was. When I asked Him for help, He said, "Who do you want to be?" This confused me until He added, "Who you want to be is who you really are. That is why you want to be that way."

Religion teaches us to not trust our instincts. Our instincts tell us that an abundant life would include a sense of fulfillment in doing what we were individually born to do, according to the gifts within us. For some, this is something creative like dance, art, or design. For others, it is teaching, researching, writing, or other endless possibilities. Too often we are asking God to show us what to do with our lives, while we hide our innate talents (or "die to them"), thinking that anything we enjoy must not be of God. Religion has generally made people feel that the only godly occupation is something done within the confines of a church or mission field. Many think the only time they please God is when they are within the church walls or doing ministry work like feeding the poor, witnessing, or having devotions. I disagree. I believe if we are given a talent and a desire to build things, decorate homes or design huge structures, then it is our destiny to do it unto the Lord.

Did you ever think that art or a well-designed room is a tool God uses to restore your soul? In the Old Testament, God anointed the artisans for His temple (Exodus 31:5-7). I think He is also anointing artisans for His footstool (Matthew 5:35) so let's allow Him to anoint the artisans of the world. Let's release Him into our workplaces, not just to witness or model character, but also to glorify Him with our talents.

The main point I hope to make in sharing all this is that God wants us to give His Spirit a voice; His voice is not just words, but includes sounds, actions, dance, art, and anything that expresses His creative and diverse presence. To do this, we must come alive to what He has created us to be so that He is glorified, and we live a life of abundance!

APPLICATION

Write down three things that you enjoy doing. How can you glorify God through them? Write down who you want to be – not titles or positions but personality, gifts, or talents. (*Note: I thought I desired to be musical because I loved to worship. I did not get passionate enough to learn to sing or play an instrument, but I did spend a lot of time in His presence and realized it was not the playing or singing that was my real goal, but the worship!*)

DECLARATION

God wants me to live an abundant life and use the talents He has given me that bring me energy and fulfillment.

INNER UNITY

*"That they all may be one, as You, Father, are in Me, and I in You;
that they also may be one in Us, that the world may
believe that You sent Me."*

John 17:21

One day as I was praying for unity in the church, God threw out a comment that has impacted my thought life tremendously. He said, "Wendy, if you could just get in unity with yourself, you could change the world." Until that moment, I had not considered the thought that I was not in inner unity. But as He spoke, I realized that if my thoughts, emotions, words, and prayers were not unified, then perhaps my conscious beliefs had not meshed with my unconscious beliefs.

Amazingly, I began seeing the measure of unity within myself directly impacting my level of influence in the natural and spiritual realms. It also revealed to me why some of the promises of God that

I had been declaring were not manifesting. For instance, for many years I never experienced the promise of 2 Corinthians 9:8 to walk in abundance for every good work. I tithed, gave, sacrificed, and was a good steward, yet I still lived from miracle to miracle, barely getting by. I got caught in the trap of thinking something was wrong with me or I couldn't be trusted with riches. I reverted to a performance mentality that got me nowhere!

Then a revelation came to me that set me free. God very clearly said, "You are only able to receive what you think you are worth." I realized that I was unconsciously sabotaging myself and stepping out of His flow of blessing whenever the blessing outgrew my view of my worth. This was not just in the financial realm, but I discovered that I had an unspoken and unconscious measurement for how much favor, anointing, or success I deserved. I had a mental assent that I was worthy through grace to receive everything Jesus purchased on the cross, but my unconscious heart belief was not in unity with this belief.

As a newlywed, I had very low self-esteem. Although my husband continually said he loved me, I didn't really believe it in the depth of my being. His love was at odds with my belief that I was unlovable. This caused a lot of stress in our marriage. My mind always looked for proof that he didn't love me, and everything was colored by the core belief that I was unlovable. If he did dishes for me, I interpreted that to mean he thought I was a poor wife or house cleaner. Later, I discovered that doing acts of service is one of his greatest love languages, and he was trying to say "I love you" by doing the dishes. I realized my doubts were sabotaging our marriage. He was receiving signals that no matter what he did, it wouldn't be enough. Once I realized that he was not my problem, I felt empowered. I began to work on my own beliefs. I discovered my thoughts about myself were opposing the very things I wanted to receive. As I changed my self-view, my ability to receive love drastically increased.

If you have been begging and begging for a promise to manifest in your life and cannot seem to obtain it, I suggest you ask God if there is a core belief that is opposing the reception of the blessing. Too often we use outward blessings as proof of His love and our worthiness, not knowing that our negative self-evaluation can hinder the manifestation of His blessing – which we often interpret as proof that we are unlovable.

Jump off the "performance train" and spend time exploring how much He loves you. Rather than looking for proof of His love, it is important to receive His love by faith, just as you did at your salvation. Spend time meditating on His love and speaking His love over yourself. Because faith comes by hearing (Romans 10:17), begin to declare how lovely you are in His sight until everything within you believes it!

It is important to realize that there is a difference between what we want to believe and what our unconscious mind or heart really believe. The good news is that we can change what we truly believe through declarations, revelations, and encounters with God. Many of our false beliefs have been created from wrong conclusions made from past emotional experiences. For instance, when a child has something shameful done to them, they conclude that they are shameful or should be ashamed. They may live with that belief all their lives and never discover the truth behind what is driving and sabotaging their life. God desires to reveal that our identity is not decided from what has happened to us or from what we have done. Our true identity is not determined from our actions but from what God has placed within us. It is time to let go of our false conclusions and base our identity on who the Word of God says we are!

Each new encounter and revelation of His love and truth will impact how we live and see life. As we become aware and address areas of disunity within ourselves, we will eliminate the unseen limitations affecting our lives. This inner unity will empower us to live a supernatural lifestyle.

APPLICATION

What do you think holds you back from breaking out of your normal level of success in finances, relationships, jobs, spiritual growth, etc.? Ask God to reveal any false conclusions made in your past that are holding you to your present experience. Create declarations that will help change your beliefs. You might want to check and see if your words, emotions, thoughts, and prayers are in unity.

DECLARATION

I submit my mind, will, and emotions to the truth of God's Word, which says I am altogether lovely and beloved by God.

Abundant Living
three

CREATING
STRONGHOLDS

"The weapons of our warfare are not carnal but mighty in God,
for pulling down strongholds, casting down arguments and every high
thing that exalts itself against the knowledge of God,
bringing every thought into captivity."

2 Corinthians 10:4-5

I used to think this verse meant I should stop thinking evil or unkind thoughts. But I discovered that it means much more than not thinking lustful or unkind things. God doesn't want us to just take evil or perverted thoughts into captivity. He wants us to take every thought captive that exalts a person, circumstance, or emotion over God's promises. For instance, do you realize that any hopeless thought is exalting itself over the God of all hope (Romans 15:13)? He isn't against our evil thoughts because they disgust Him, but because He knows that our thoughts become fortresses and carry a force in the unseen realm that affect our everyday lives.

If we are to demolish strongholds, it might be wise to understand the meaning of the word. A stronghold is a place of defense. It is a well-fortified position that is ready to defend its right to stay and rule in a certain place. If you have a stronghold of thinking that you are always unloved or rejected, then your brain will constantly look for proof to defend that belief system. It will be blind to any circumstance that speaks of love and acceptance because that is not the belief it wants to defend. We tend to only see what we are looking for.

I used to work up the emotion of hope for hopeless circumstances because I thought it would prove that I trusted God. Every time I felt hopeless, I would try to subdue the emotion and take it captive. It was a never-ending battle of forcefully trying to subdue hopelessness. This battle reminds me of a quote I heard by Edmund Burke, an Irish statesman and philosopher from the 1700's. *"The use of force alone is but temporary. It may subdue for a moment; but it does not remove the necessity of subduing again; and a nation is not governed, which is perpetually to be conquered."* He, of course, is referring to nations, but this also applies to the "nations" of our mind and emotions. If we continue to force ourselves to have hope or "feel loved" without first changing what we truly believe, we will live in a constant battle within ourselves. We will be in a perpetual state of subduing ourselves because "forcing" the emotions of hope and faith is temporary. We do not want to subdue emotions, but we want to change the thoughts (strongholds) that are producing our emotions. *We must change the beliefs that **govern** our emotions.* If we unconsciously believe that we are unworthy to receive God's provision, then every time we pray or declare His promises for provision, a battle will ensue. A part of us will want to hope in God, and the other part, provoked by the stronghold of unworthiness, will experience the emotion of hopelessness. Instead of constantly subduing emotions, I recommend that we create new strongholds within our mind.

If we can build negative strongholds that exalt themselves against the truths of God, then we can build positive strongholds around the knowledge of His goodness, power, and love. *We can intentionally develop healthy inner strongholds for our identity, acceptance, and abilities.* How do we do this? The answer is simple. Let's take the belief that we are "favored by God and man" as an example. To build this belief as a "stronghold" in our minds, we would first need to ask God to reveal every thought that would resist this belief and ask Him to reveal the truth in each of those areas. Perhaps we would discover that we unconsciously believe we have not earned unlimited favor and therefore cannot expect it. Or perhaps we would discover that we think we can not be trusted with such favor. Or maybe we even discover that our mind has actually been rehearsing all of our past experiences that "prove" we do not have favor. Whatever the lie is that we are believing, we need to ask God to reveal His truth in that area.

To intentionally develop a healthy inner stronghold for the belief that we are "favored by God and man," we should consciously look for scripture and circumstantial proof that indicates we do have favor. We need to rehearse and declare them until a new stronghold is erected.

Instead of developing a healthy inner stronghold, most people tend to unconsciously dwell on negative events or circumstances that seem to defend their current beliefs. For example, if a man believed that his leaders did not value or trust him, then his mind would view his leaders' every action and word with the **intent** of proving that belief. I recommend that people purposely look for proof of the opposite stronghold. Start looking for proof that you are valued and trusted. I would encourage this man to write down everything that could remotely be construed as value or trust. By changing what we look for, we radically affect our relationships with both God and man. Take time every day to find proof of your new belief system or stronghold.

I try to be intentional about developing and establishing new specific strongholds. I once spent a year on a quest to understand the goodness of God. I did this because I needed to break a religious stronghold that I had developed which perverted the concept of God's goodness. For years, I thought that the goodness of God meant that God did bad things to me for my good. I thought He only trained through pain. I even thought He would kill my husband so I could grow in Christian character. This warped view of the goodness of God severely affected my ability to trust Him and enjoy the life He purchased for me.

When God revealed the meaning of Romans 2:4 to me, which says, *"The goodness of God leads [us] to repentance,"* my whole world was transformed. When I made this belief a stronghold in my life, it transformed what I expected from both God and life. One thing I have noticed is that Biblical information is not revelation until it changes our view of life. Revelation should change our response and emotions without any effort on our part. Whether they are based on truth or lies, strongholds engender emotions without effort. For example, if I believe I am stupid, how hard do you think I would have to work in order to stimulate feelings of stupidity or humiliation? Usually, it would take no effort at all! This is great news, because if it works in the negative, we can be sure it will work in the positive! By taking truths that we intellectually believe, and making them into strongholds through declaring, meditating, and receiving revelation, we can be sure that new, healthy responses and emotions will automatically follow!

APPLICATION

What emotion do you continually have to subdue in order for it to line up with the truth? Write down the belief that is governing the emotion and put it inside a covered jar as a prophetic act. Then write the truth and begin declaring, meditating, and receiving revelation for this new chosen stronghold.

DECLARATION

New positive strongholds are making life easy!

SUPERNATURAL LAWS

"For the law of the Spirit of life in Christ Jesus has made me free from the law of sin and death."

Romans 8:2

It amazes me how often we live our lives based on the laws of this natural realm. Let me illustrate this by using a law most of us are familiar with: the law of gravity. We understand that the law of gravity will work for everyone even if they have never heard of it or believe in it. What is even more amazing, is that there is a law that supersedes the law of gravity: the law of lift. The law of lift allows airplanes to defy the law of gravity and fly. The law of lift does not nullify the law of gravity, but it supersedes it. Romans 1:20 tells us God is revealed through the natural realm; therefore, it is only reasonable to assume that what works in the natural realm has a mirror image in the unseen realm. This truth helps us to understand that although there is the law of judgment, there is another law that can supersede it: the law of mercy. Again, the law of mercy, which is what we see at work on the cross, does not nullify the law of judgment, but it does supersede it.

As partakers of the divine nature and citizens of the kingdom, we must realize that the spiritual laws of the kingdom are higher than the natural laws of our planet. This is why our hope should not be based on circumstances, performance, or an event, but based on core values derived from the Word (such as Romans 8:28, which states that eventually everything works out for our good, because we are called according to His purpose). Even in the midst of trials, I know that goodness and mercy are about to catch up with me, because they have been following me all the days of my life (Psalm 23).

As we have been discussing laws superseding other laws, I want to point out something very important: We never live in denial to an inferior law because real faith is not living in denial. We are not pretending that a problem or law does not exist. Genuine faith does not deny the facts about our circumstances, but it believes God's goodness and promises will supersede the "facts" for our benefit. Romans 4:18-21 illustrates this – when Abraham hoped against all hope by not considering his aged body or the deadness of Sarah's womb, but believed what God had said. In other words, he was not focused on the natural laws of aging but on the supernatural ability of God's promises to supersede those laws.

When Ezekiel looked at the valley of dry bones in Ezekiel 37, he did not go into denial. He admitted they were very dry, but he did not say they could not live! He refused to make a conclusion based on his past experiences with bones or the apparent impossibility. Common sense and scientific laws would tell us those bones would never live again; however, with God there is a higher law than the law of death – the law of life (Romans 8:2)!

In order for us to live a victorious life, it is vital for us to understand how the unseen realm works. Many believers are still trying to manifest the unseen realm through the Old Testament method of works and performance, and do not understand that as soon as they try to obtain the Spirit realm through performance, they are cutting themselves off from grace, or divine empowerment. Most Christians seem to think that sinful actions cause us to fall from grace, but that is not true. Galatians 5:4 says, *"You who attempt to be justified by law; you have fallen from grace."* This means that it is not wrong conduct that causes us to fall from grace, but a performance or works mentality. The Greek word for grace in Galatians 5:4 is *charis*, which means *"divine influence, good will or favor toward."* This means that if we try to become accepted through performance, we automatically are disqualified from the divine influence that can enable us to be changed. The revelation that Jesus has already made us holy and supernatural will cause the manifestation of holiness through us. This explains why many Christians are not flowing in the promises of God – they are invoking an inferior spiritual law that is working against them.

For too many years, I thought that God was capricious and unstable in how He answered prayer and decided what to do in my life. Finally, I began to understand that most of what was happening was actually determined by spiritual laws, not necessarily God's sovereign choices. If this is hard to wrap your mind around, my husband actually wrote a book on this topic entitled *Divine Strategies*. We need to understand how things work in His kingdom before we make conclusions about His character based on our experiences.

For example, if you lack finances, you may have concluded it is His will for you to be in lack. But actually, the lack of finances may be caused by the belief that you are not worthy of blessing, not because of God's desire for you to be poor. Fear (faith for bad to happen) may also be a reason you have not seen breakthrough manifest. Trust me, God's promises come when we embrace the reality of God's spiritual laws.

The Christian life is a journey of discovering God's character and the mysteries of the kingdom that govern our experience. God is a God of order. He is not whimsical or unstable. We must begin to understand the spiritual laws that govern His Kingdom and align ourselves to them.

APPLICATION

Think about an area of your life that consistently seems untouched by God's grace. Ask God if there is a spiritual law at work that is hindering breakthrough in this area. Do not seek to hear out of fear, but believe that He will give you the wisdom you need. Rest and listen with peaceful expectation. Believe that He awakens your ear to hear Him (Isaiah 50:5).

DECLARATION

I have great revelation about
how the laws of the spirit realm work.

five

MYSTERIES OF
THE KINGDOM

"To you it has been given to know the mysteries of the kingdom of God,
but to the rest it is given in parables,
that 'Seeing they may not see,
And hearing they may not understand.'"

Luke 8:10

This scripture is an obvious invitation to search out the hidden mysteries of the Kingdom. To do that, we must first believe that we can see and hear beyond the *natural* ability of our eyes and ears. First Corinthians 4:1-3 says we are stewards of the mysteries of God. What is it that we are stewarding? Two chapters before, in 1 Corinthians 2:11-13, we find that we have received the Spirit from God. Without the Spirit, or shall I say the "eyes of the Spirit," we cannot see the mysteries of what is in the Kingdom or how it functions. The rest of this verse says, *"So that we might know the things freely given to us by God."* Again, this is a clear invitation to search out the hidden mysteries of the Kingdom. Learning to steward the mysteries of the Kingdom requires us to **see life through the eyes and resources of the spirit realm.** As you begin to do this, your spirit will begin to show you things that your natural eye cannot see or hear.

According to Colossians 1:13, we have already been translated into God's Kingdom. This is wonderful news! Now, we must learn how His Kingdom functions, just as man has been learning the ways of this natural realm throughout the ages. For instance, man has discovered how germs affect our bodies, how the moon affects the tides, how vitamins affect our health, and so on. Learning the mysteries of the Kingdom will also be an ongoing process as we, the people of God, respond to the invitation to search out His mysteries.

Acknowledging that His Kingdom has laws that are new to us and that govern our lives will enable us to recognize that our old version of reality has to be adjusted. Consider Joshua and Caleb in Numbers 13. Unlike the other ten spies, Joshua and Caleb did not look at the Promised Land according to the natural laws, but through the spiritual eyes of the promises of God. Or consider the miracle in John 2. According to the known laws of nature, water will never turn into wine; but in John 2, Jesus caused this change to happen by operating out of kingdom principles that are mysterious to the world.

Most of us are conditioned to determine *reality* through our natural senses, and then react in what seems to be the most logical manner. This did not work out well for the ten spies who reported to the Children of Israel. It is interesting that they saw the exact same set of circumstances as Joshua and Caleb, yet came up with a different report. Joshua and Caleb did not deny the presence of giants or the reality of the difficulties, but they saw something in the unseen realm that the others were unable to see. They understood that the invisible realities have a greater influence than the realities of the natural realm. The ten spies based their conclusions on the resources of this natural realm, while Joshua and Caleb based their conclusions on the resources and promises of heaven. Joshua and Caleb probably had people telling them to "face reality" or to "be realistic." When people tell me they are "just being realistic," I like to remind them that they are not called to be realistic, but to be supernatural!

When I first started speaking in public, my main focus was on my ability to put thoughts together and speak with clarity, but then I heard someone say that there was coming a day that the anointing of God would be so tangible that we could say "peanut butter" and people would cry out "What must we do to be saved?" It may sound strange, but when I heard that, I literally felt something shift in my brain. The thought came to me that when I speak in public, my faith should be in God's ability to anoint my words – not my great ability to speak. This thought released me from the fear of performing well, and set my eyes on the unseen substance of God's realm. Like Joshua and Caleb, I saw that I could overcome the giant of poor speaking by placing my faith in the unseen realm and promises of God.

Many Christians believe that walking in the spirit (Galatians 5) means not doing fleshly activities. They live a life of good works and subconsciously believe that it will invoke a law of the spirit that will bring success; however, Hebrews 11:6 says that *without faith it is impossible to please Him.* Faith is the *mystery of the Kingdom* that actually pleases God and invokes the *law* of success. Many confuse obedience with faith, and when their obedient actions fail to bring success, they get confused. Let me explain what I mean by this with an illustration. If I tell others about Jesus only out of obedience, I may never see anyone saved. I may be witnessing to please God, but I may have a belief system that says "No one wants to be saved in my region." My beliefs affect how people respond to my witnessing efforts. Although people may occasionally get saved purely from my obedience, even more will be saved through the long term effects of changing what I believe about witnessing.

When something fails or goes wrong, how often do we first look at what we did or how we did it for the resolution? Perhaps we should ask ourselves, "What did I believe when I did it?"

It is important to become aware of the unconscious beliefs that are directing our lives, because oftentimes they are not based on scriptural truths but on religious traditions. When we attach faith to His promises, then we can factor those promises into our circumstances and come up with new *possible* results for *impossible* circumstances.

APPLICATION

Look at an impossible circumstance through the eyes of the spirit. What are some promises that can be applied to the circumstance? Apply the promises and allow the Holy Spirit to paint a picture of new possible results.

DECLARATION

I have unseen resources and spiritual blessings to
overcome every negative circumstance.

GODLY IMAGINATION

For most of my Christian life, I thought my imagination was evil and a tool for the devil. Then God revealed to me that He created my imagination for a purpose, and the purpose is not to give the devil a playground.

Mark 4:14 calls the "Word" a "seed." This spiritual seed is not just for salvation, but is a seed that brings healing, encouragement, deliverance, and provision. I believe that God wants us to plant the promises of His Word as seeds into our hearts. We then take these "seeds" and meditate and imagine the promises at work in our lives. **It is in our imagination that we conceive these things and frame up our future.** However, many of us after receiving a seed continue to imagine our circumstance without the fruit of the seed. God plants a seed of provision, but we water, nourish, and conceive lack because that is what we allow our imaginations to envision.

The imagination is the womb for the seed of either God's Word or satan's thoughts. Is it any wonder that the enemy wants to have access to our imaginations? If the enemy can use our imaginations, then how much more can God?

What do you imagine or think about when you are tired and not thinking on purpose? Maybe you need to repent (change the way you think) in order to change what you are birthing.

I declare revelation as you read this next section on how to use your godly imagination.

Godly Imagination

one

FIX
YOUR EYE

"So we fix our eyes not on what is seen, but on what is unseen.
For what is seen is temporary, but what is unseen is eternal."

2 Corinthians 4:18 NIV

Once, while meditating on this verse, I tried to fix my eye on what was unseen – but how does someone stare at a realm that is invisible? I realized that to see something beyond the natural, I would need to use my imagination. The imagination is a place where God can paint a picture of the heavenly realm (spiritual realm) or of the future.

I have heard it said that worry is fellowshipping with the devil. In other words, worry is allowing the enemy to paint a picture in our imagination of what could happen in the future. He may cause us to see ourselves failing or being inadequate in the things we desire to do, or he may create a picture of the consequences of failing, like being rejected or humiliated. He wants us to imagine what will happen if we lack money, approval, time, wisdom, etc. Our brain attaches faith to whatever it sees or thinks is true. So, when we have a picture in our mind, we will unconsciously attach faith to whatever we have seen. This is why the devil wants to play the "what if" game in our minds.

I challenge you to play the "what if" game with God instead. This is a game where we allow God to paint a picture in our minds of what is possible under His blessing and anointing. For instance, when my husband and I play this game, we will say things like "What if God provides us with so much money that we have to hire someone to help us give it away?" or "What if every time we go to the store, people follow us around crying, 'What must we do to be saved?'" or "What if our anointing gets so strong that people accidentally get healed when we walk down the street?" I find it fascinating that it is so easy to imagine ourselves in difficulty and lack instead of abundance and victory.

People may resist playing the "what if" game out of fear of being prideful. Some people believe that imagining ourselves as successful, strong, or influential is considered vain imagining and pride. This limits us from manifesting the power of God through us. It is time to stop being afraid of success and start imagining ourselves as shining for God!

Émile Coué de Châtaigneraie (1857-1926), a French psychologist, once said, *"When the imagination and willpower are in conflict, **it is always the imagination which wins, without any exception.**"* This explains why many of us are failing to accomplish what we "will" to do. Perhaps you have the will to quit a habit but have not succeeded because you cannot imagine yourself free from the power of that addiction. I believe the ability to do the impossible will be released when we allow God to use our imaginations in order for us to see prophetically (according to His power and promises). We have to see His power working in us and through us, enabling us to do the impossible.

Begin to imagine your future according to His power at work within you. See yourself as an overcomer, as a new creation, as righteous or as successful at whatever you put your hand to. Read Deuteronomy 28 and 30 to get a picture of what a righteous person looked like under the Old Covenant. Imagine how much more blessed you are because of what Christ accomplished on the cross.

See yourself through the eyes of faith, not through the veil of the past. Remember that faith is not blind but it is *visionary*, which is, according to Encarta World English Dictionary, *"characterized by unusually acute foresight and imagination."*

Can you allow your imagination to see life according to the power within you?

APPLICATION

Think of an area that you have tried to change through will power. Spend a few minutes imagining the power of God over that area. Now write down what God revealed is possible through His power working in and through you.

DECLARATION

The eyes of my imagination are enlightened to see the glorious inheritance and power that I have been called into (Ephesians 1:18,19).

two

DIMENSIONS OF THE MIND
Part One

"There he built an altar, and he called the place El Bethel, because it was there that God revealed himself to him."

Genesis 35:7

I love considering how the mind works and how to make it work for us, rather than against us. God created the mind to serve us, not to keep us in captivity. Two of the main dimensions of the mind are memory and imagination. God created these functions to bless us and cause us to prosper. Unfortunately, the enemy has used these gifts against us. It is time that we stop making our memory and imagination tools for the enemy and begin using them for their original intent.

First, I want to address the function of memory. Our memory enables us to remember the things of the past and the things we have learned. Regrettably, many of us rehearse the memories of our failures and remind ourselves of what we haven't learned! We tend to make altars to our failures rather than altars to His faithfulness. Too often, we sit and meditate on our failures and imperfections. We may bring these things to remembrance because we think it is the responsible and righteous thing to do. And while it may be helpful to learn from our past, most of us do not really receive constructive help from reliving our past. Instead, we are unconsciously punishing ourselves for not measuring up. We do not overcome sin because we are perpetually spending time grieving over it. We overcome sin by focusing on what Jesus purchased for us, which is a new nature and total acceptance from the Heavenly Father.

As a young Christian, I used to lie in bed each night rehearsing everything I did wrong that day. It felt spiritual to meditate on my failures. Then one night, I heard God say, "Wendy, why are you building altars to your failures?" That question prompted me to realize that scripturally, people never built altars or memorial stones to remind them of their failures. They only built them around their victories and successes. I now encourage people to dwell on what they have done right and see what happens.

One thing I have noticed is when I dwell on my failures, I am robbed of energy and motivation; however, when I dwell on my successes, I am energized and motivated to attempt more. We must be aware of our emotional and physical responses to the thought we choose to dwell on. Are our thoughts draining us or causing hopelessness? If so, then we must change our perspective by seeing what God is saying about the situation. His voice never carries hopelessness, condemnation, or lack of energy. He is never hopeless. He never condemns or drains us of energy. He is the opposite of those things. He is the God of all hope who promises us that there is now no condemnation for those who are in Christ. He cannot drain us because He is the One who fills us with joy and peace (Romans 15:13). Are your thoughts bringing you hope and filling you with the divine energy of life or are they generating emotional fruit incongruent with God's character? The answer is vital to our becoming all that we can be in Christ.

Many believers think it is prideful to meditate on our success and victories. **But if remembering our failures is so helpful, then why are we not made perfect through remembrance of sins rather than the forgiveness of sins?** If we would spend more time making altars of remembrance to our testimonies and His promises, we would see more long lasting effects in our character and life.

In Genesis 35, it is interesting that when Jacob built the altar at Bethel, it was built on a revelation he wanted to remember. I think the revelation was not just a revelation about God's nature, but of how God saw him. It was a reminder that his name was no longer Jacob the deceiver, but Israel, the prince with God.

It is time to build altars of remembrance by spending time meditating on and remembering the testimonies of His grace and goodness towards us. Also, we should remember we are no longer sinners but saints; and no longer slaves to sin, but empowered by grace.

Take note of your emotions when thinking about yourself. If the fruit of those thoughts are always hopelessness, a lack of strength, or condemnation, then your thoughts about yourself are not based on your biblical identity. Correct thinking will always produce fruits of the Spirit. Good altars will produce hope, peace, joy, etc.

What kind of altars have you built in your mind? Do you have a past experience that has become an altar of remembrance? We know we have built an altar around a past experience when it still influences our thinking today. If a negative past experience has more power in determining your emotions or future than God's Word, then it is time to tear that altar down and build a new one.

APPLICATION

Build an altar today around a successful past experience that reveals how God has changed you or helped you. Create a journal of successes. Celebrate seemingly small things like saying no to cake, speaking well of someone, declaring God's Word, or praying for ten minutes.

DECLARATION

I succeed in everything I put my hand to.

three

DIMENSIONS
OF THE MIND
Part Two

*"Finally, brothers and sisters, whatever is true, whatever is noble,
whatever is right, whatever is pure, whatever is lovely,
whatever is admirable—if anything is excellent or praiseworthy—
think about such things."*

Philippians 4:8 NIV

As I mentioned before, two of the main functions of the mind are the ability to remember and imagine. We will now consider the imagination dimension. After studying about the imagination, I am still fascinated that various dictionaries make a connection between the following words: imagination, creative power, vision and inspiration. Could this mean that creative power, vision, and inspiration are linked to what we are imagining?

Many times we do the opposite of Philippians 4:8. We meditate on our failures and things that are wrong or we think on things that inspire us into hopelessness or pain. I discovered that when a passing thought becomes a focus in my mind, my imagination will build a picture (framework) for that thought. Then I discovered that my brain was like a muscle that could be trained to hold certain thoughts and reject others. This truth helped me to understand that I was not a victim to my thoughts. In fact, it brought hope because I discovered that through godly meditation, I could change the way I think.

Think of your brain not just as an organ for thinking, but as a radio receiver that picks up different stations (according to what the radio receiver is tuned into). For most of my life, my brain was tuned into the enemy's station. I constantly heard an inner voice telling me I was inadequate, unimportant, and unlovable. My imagination built pictures of apparent proof that these thoughts were true. Eventually, thoughts that we continually tune into will become our own beliefs, not just passing thoughts.

Just as we question which thoughts are of God and which are our own, we should consider whether thoughts are the enemy's or ours. More importantly, we should be thinking on *purpose* as Philippians 4:8 says, rather than being victims of the "airwaves." To think on purpose means that I am not just playing defense (rejecting negative thoughts), but I am actually on offense (*purposely* deciding what I want to think about).

The ability to remember and imagine was created by God to enable us to prosper; therefore, we need to intentionally use these gifts in a healthy way, designed by God. Unfortunately, we tend to imagine our future based on the memories of our past. For most of us, this is not good news! For instance, if we failed or humiliated ourselves in a past circumstance, then in similar future circumstances, we will produce the same result. Often we draw the wrong conclusions based on past experiences. For example, the first time I spoke in front of a small group of people, I stood up, started to cry and could not talk. I sat down and thought, "I will never speak in front of people again." That painful memory, and other similar failures, haunted me. I used to rehearse these failures before I got up to speak, and every time, I continued to fail. Because I had failed in the past, I had drawn a conclusion that I could not speak in front of crowds. But then, under the anointing, I started to imagine myself as a successful public speaker having favor as I spoke. This caused things to radically change.

What would happen to a baby if he assumed he could not walk, talk or feed himself based on his past experience? He would assume he did not have the "gift" of walking or talking. And if the baby had tried and failed, he would use the failure as proof that those gifts were not in his DNA; however, babies instinctively know that they should not look to their past for their identity or capabilities, but they look to their parents for these things. As born again children of God, we also should be looking to our Father to determine who and what we are.

God told me once that I could no longer create my identity from my past but only from my future. I was to be like a child that looked to its parents to see its potential and abilities. So instead of getting my identity from what I was, I had to focus on what I was becoming.

In order to live from our future and receive the full benefit of how God created us, we need to take advantage of the power of imagination. We can do this by allowing God to paint a picture of our future as a supernatural being (not just picturing what job we will have or what we may own, although that may be included). See yourself enslaved to righteousness, successful in everything you do, full of favor, wisdom, power, and confidence. Imagine yourself able to change atmospheres and seeing sickness and demons flee from the glory of God that you carry. In other words look at your Daddy, and "see" your future.

Seeing ourselves according to our future is very important, but it is not as important as believing we are already carrying the DNA to accomplish that future. Studies have shown that wealthy people do not think they are wealthy because they have money, but they think they have money because they are wealthy. That is why millionaires can lose all their money and become millionaires again and again. They believe who they are on the inside is what makes them successful on the outside.

Albert Einstein (1879-1955) wrote, "*Imagination is more important than knowledge. For knowledge is limited to all we now know and understand, while imagination embraces the entire world, and all there ever will be to know and understand.*"

APPLICATION

Take one aspect of God that His Spirit highlights to you and imagine yourself walking in it until that picture eclipses your past experience. For instance, consider God's resurrection power. Picture the same Spirit that raised Christ from the dead dwelling in you. How would that affect sickness in you or in someone else? How would that affect your tiredness or depression? How would that affect your city?

DECLARATION

I know my past, but I imagine my future
according to the power that works in me.

four

ATTACHING FAITH

*"And not being weak in faith, he did not consider his own body,
already dead (since he was about a hundred years old),
and the deadness of Sarah's womb. He did not waver at the
promise of God through unbelief, but was strengthened in faith,
giving glory to God, and being fully convinced that what
He had promised He was also able to perform."*

Romans 4:19-21

I love how God speaks to me. He will drop a thought in my mind and then wait to see if I will be noble enough to search out all the riches within that thought (Proverbs 25:2). One of the most wealthy thoughts that has come to me is "I do not need to do anything different. I just need to attach great faith to what I am already doing." This powerful truth has two aspects that I want to discuss.

The first is learning to recognize what kind of faith we are unconsciously attaching to our actions, circumstances, or people.

This was made real to me one day while getting ready for a counseling session with a certain person. I was dreading the meeting, and God asked me why. I explained to Him that the person I was meeting with was not very teachable and was very prone to defensiveness and anger. In short, I was expecting very negative results from this meeting. God then quietly said, "If that is your faith for this appointment, I do not want you to go." I was stunned because I knew He was not telling me not to go, but to change my faith for the meeting. In order to do that, I had to "see" differently. When I became receptive to seeing the meeting through the eyes of my spirit, I realized I had limited the meeting to the natural realm. He began to remind me that I carried a spirit of revelation that could influence her thoughts and emotions. I was able to see myself walking in the substance of love and grace, which would enable her to feel accepted and teachable. Wow! Once I saw the potential for the meeting, I got excited and attached great faith to what would be accomplished. As a result, it was a great meeting!

Now when I have feelings of dread, I recognize that I have attached negative beliefs to the situation. Too often, we accept feelings of dread because it seems reasonable. But it is just a signal that we have made conclusions based on the natural realm rather than the supernatural. This principle is not just for things that seem spiritual. For instance, soon after the counseling meeting that I mentioned above, God asked me why I often procrastinated and dreaded vacuuming my carpet. I thought about it and became aware that I believed vacuuming was time consuming and hard. This belief was based on my unpleasant experience as a young girl vacuuming our large family home. I purposely began changing my belief about vacuuming. I began to see it as easy. When I actually timed myself, I discovered that (in the house I lived in) it only took ten minutes! I also began using the time while vacuuming to pray in the spirit and began to love it! This experience taught me that just because something feels true, it does not mean it is true.

Changing what you believe about something will change the feelings attached to it. Are you dreading a meeting, a responsibility or even an entire day? Ask God to show you what belief has caused this dread. Then allow Him to show you what it can look like through the eyes of your spirit. As we learn to recognize when we are attaching negative faith to our life, it can be a fun adventure. I love the results of freedom from dread to life!

The other aspect of attaching faith is training ourselves to expect great results from small actions. Many people are waiting for an opportunity to do great things for God, but He is waiting for us to do small things with great faith. What do you have in your hand? What can you do now? For instance, if you clean houses for a living, attach outrageous faith to what you do. Start believing that you leave a substance of love and joy in the homes you clean. Prophesy encounters and dreams over the people who sleep on the sheets you put on the beds. Impart health and healing into the towels you fold or the dishes you clean.

If you play a musical instrument, you are not only playing notes to make a pleasant sound or simply backing up a worship team. Start attaching faith to different notes or sounds. Believe some notes are setting people free, some are sounds bringing healing, and some are shifting atmospheres. Remember, David's harp brought relief and caused evil spirits to leave Saul in 1 Samuel 16:23.

Often, as Christians we expect negative results from the acts of witches or sinful people in regions, but do not understand the impact from the righteous acts of people in an area. If we believe that witches can create strongholds, or that consistent sin creates strongholds in lives or regions, then we must believe that every time we worship or take communion, we are building strongholds in our lives and cities. I believe that if we attach faith to such things as consistent acts of kindness or blessings, then they should have even more impact than acts of sin or curses.

Attaching godly faith to our lives means we will have to spend more time asking God what life looks like when it is subject to the Kingdom of our God. Attaching faith means we will see life differently and have different expectations from familiar actions.

APPLICATION

Write down some simple things you do every day and dream with God about the powerful effects it can have because of Christ living in you. Write down some declarations based on what God shows you concerning these simple things.

DECLARATION

I attach great faith to everything I do;
therefore, everything I do creates life and change.

CONCLUDING REFLECTIONS

Although this book has come to a close, I know that your journey has only begun. Jesus said, *"For whoever has, to him more will be given"* (Mark 4:25). In other words, the more understanding we receive, the more that will be given. Each new truth becomes a launching pad for the next revelation (line upon line). I bless you with eyes that see the unseen realities of the kingdom. My prayer is that this book will lead you into even greater truths, that will in turn benefit the whole body of Christ.

The things I have shared in this book were not revelations that I received in one day and instantly bore fruit. I had to apply these revelations and make them my new lens for viewing life. Through long-term declarations and meditation, I was able to get these truths into the spirit of my mind. At first, it can be hard to challenge our old beliefs and feelings, but I want to encourage you that it will get easier!

I believe that consistently rereading portions of this book that the Spirit highlights will accelerate the process of renewing your mind and changing the way you see life. It is not enough that your intellect understands something. I often will listen to certain messages five times a day, because I want the truth to go past my intellect and into my spirit. The goal is to understand and believe with the spirit of our minds.

When reading, listening, or seeing something that causes your spirit to leap, then you should search it out. Spend time meditating on it and asking God questions. Recognize that your spirit is trying to teach your brain something. I hope that you will be challenged by thoughts in this book that will cause your spirit to leap and your mind to be renewed so that your life will be transformed.

By the grace of God, I believe that this book will be a catalyst for opening blind eyes. In the name of Jesus, I impart fresh grace for you to live from the unseen realm, and I pray for His Kingdom to manifest more fully in your life.

Blessings on your journey!

Wendy

IGNITING HOPE
RESOURCES

Victorious Mindsets

What we believe is ultimately more important than what we do. The course of our lives is set by our deepest core beliefs. Our mindsets are either a stronghold for God's purposes or a playhouse for the enemy. In this book, fifty biblical attitudes are revealed that are foundational for those who desire to walk in freedom and power.

Cracks in the Foundation

Going to a higher level in establishing key beliefs will affect one's intimacy with God and fruitfulness for the days ahead. This book challenges many basic assumptions of familiar Bible verses and common Christian phrases that block numerous benefits of our salvation. The truths shared in this book will help fill and repair "cracks" in our thinking which rob us of our God-given potential.

You're Crazy If You Don't Talk to Yourself

Jesus did not just think His way out of the wilderness and neither can we. He spoke truth to invisible beings and mindsets that sought to restrict and defeat Him. This book reveals that life and death are truly in the power of the tongue and emphasize the necessity of speaking truth to our souls. Our words really do set the course of our lives and the lives of others. (Proverbs 18:21)

Let's Just Laugh at That

Our hope level is an indicator of whether we are believing truth or lies. Truth creates hope and freedom, but believing lies brings hopelessness and restriction. We can have great theology but still be powerless because of deception about the key issues of life. Many of these self-defeating mindsets exist in our subconscious and have never been identified. This book exposes numerous falsehoods and reveals truth that makes us free. Get ready for a joy-infused adventure into hope-filled living.

Audio message series are available through the Igniting Hope store at:
shop-ihm.ibethel.org

Divine Strategies for Increase

The laws of the spirit are more real than the natural laws. God's laws are primarily principles to release blessing, not rules to be obeyed to gain right standing with God. The Psalmist talks of one whose greatest delight is in the law of the Lord. This delight allows one to discover new aspects of the nature of God (hidden in each law) to behold and worship. The end result of this delighting is a transformed life that prospers in every endeavor. His experience can be our experience, and this book unlocks the blessings hidden in the spiritual realm.

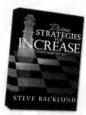

Possessing Joy

In His presence is fullness of joy (Psalm 16:11). Joy is to increase as we go deeper in our relationship with God. Religious tradition has devalued the role that gladness and laughter have for personal victory and kingdom advancement. His presence may not always produce joy, but if we never or rarely have fullness of joy, we must reevaluate our concept of God. This book takes one on a journey toward the headwaters of the full joy that Jesus often spoke of. Get ready for joy to increase and strength and longevity to ignite.

Igniting Faith in 40 Days

There must be special seasons in our lives when we break out of routine and do something that will ignite our faith about God and our identity in Christ. This book will lead you through the life-changing experience of a 40-day negativity fast. This fast teaches the power of declaring truth and other transforming daily customs that will strengthen your foundation of faith and radically increase your personal hope.

Higher Perspectives

The Bible introduces us to people who saw life's circumstances from a heavenly perspective. They were not "realistic," but supernatural in their viewpoint. As a result, they became history makers. Their experience is an invitation for us to live and see as they did. This book reveals fifty scriptural higher perspectives that will jolt you out of low-level thinking and increase your capacity to experience all of the promises of God in your life.

21397377R00069

Printed in Great Britain
by Amazon